NEW TESTAMENT
STORIES

Published by
The Church of Jesus Christ of Latter-day Saints
Salt Lake City, Utah

Copyright © 1980 Corporation
of the President of
The Church of Jesus Christ of Latter-day Saints
All Rights Reserved
Printed in United States of America

CONTENTS

ABBREVIATIONS USED IN THIS BOOK

D&C: Doctrine and Covenants

DNTC: *Doctrinal New Testament Commentary,* by Bruce R. McConkie, 3 volumes (Salt Lake City: Bookcraft, 1965-73)

JC: *Jesus the Christ,* by James E. Talmage, 3rd edition (Salt Lake City: The Church of Jesus Christ of Latter-day Saints, 1916)

JST: Joseph Smith Translation of the Bible

MD: *Mormon Doctrine,* by Bruce R. McConkie, 2nd edition (Salt Lake City: Bookcraft, 1966)

TPJS: *Teachings of the Prophet Joseph Smith,* selected by Joseph Fielding Smith (Salt Lake City: Deseret Book Co. 1938)

INTRODUCTION

To the Reader

This book will help you read and understand some of the stories from the New Testament. These stories are taken from a book that is sacred. As you read these stories, remember they are about real people who lived long ago.

Read the stories over and over until you know them well. You will also want to read them from the Bible. Under each picture you will see where you can find that story in the Bible. Have your father, mother, teacher, or friend help you.

If you do not know a word, look it up in "Words to Know" at the back of the book. If you do not know a person or place, look it up in "People to Know" or "Places to Know" at the back of the book.

To Parents and Teachers

This book will help you teach the scriptures. The "Words to Know," "People to Know," and "Places to Know" sections will help you teach the meanings of words in this book and the identity of New Testament people and places. Other helps in this book include the maps, which will also help you to help those whom you teach.

As you teach, share your testimony of the Bible. Encourage those whom you teach to seek prayerfully their own testimonies. Their understanding will grow when you read to them their favorite stories from the Bible itself.

If you are using this volume to teach the handicapped, you may be encouraged by the words of the Prophet Joseph Smith: "All the minds and spirits that God ever sent into the world are susceptible of enlargement" (TPJS, p. 354).

You may want to obtain a copy of *Teaching the Handicapped* (PBIC0187), a self-instructional in-service course, to help you develop your teaching skills. This course is available at the Salt Lake City Distribution Center, 1999 West 1700 South, Salt Lake City, Utah 84104.

You may also want to obtain *Book of Mormon Stories* (PBIC0325), and *Gospel Principles* (PBIC0245), also available at the Salt Lake City Distribution Center. *Gospel Principles* might be especially helpful in explaining doctrines such as the Fall and the Atonement.

BEFORE THE NEW TESTAMENT

We lived in heaven before we came to earth. We lived with our Heavenly Father. We were his spirit children. We had spirit bodies. We loved Heavenly Father. He loved us. He wanted us to be like him.

TPJS, p. 354

Heavenly Father had a plan. It was the plan of salvation. People who followed this plan would become like Heavenly Father. The plan said we had to come to earth. We had to get bodies of flesh and blood. We had to be tested. We had to show if we would obey God's commandments.

Abraham 3:24-25; MD, p. 520

We would go back to Heavenly Father if we obeyed him. But we would need help to go back. We would have to have our sins taken away. We would need resurrected bodies. But we could not take away our own sins. We could not resurrect our own bodies. We needed a Savior. A Savior does for us what we cannot do for ourselves. A Savior would take away our sins. A Savior would help us to be resurrected.

2 Nephi 2:5-9; MD, p. 513

Heavenly Father chose Jesus to be our Savior. Jesus loved Heavenly Father. He loved us. He wanted to be our Savior. Jesus would come to earth to save us. He would show us how to be righteous. He would suffer to take away people's sins. He would die and be resurrected. Then we could be resurrected too.

Moses 4:1-2; 2 Nephi 2:8-10

Satan also wanted to be chosen. But Satan did not love Heavenly Father. He did not love us. He wanted to change Heavenly Father's plan. He wanted Heavenly Father's power.

Moses 4:1-4.

Some of the spirits followed Satan. They did not obey God. God was very sad. He sent Satan and the spirits who followed Satan out of heaven. Satan is the devil. He and his spirits tempt us. They tell us to sin.

Moses 4:3-4

Heavenly Father told Jesus to make an earth for us. Jesus made the earth. He put plants and animals on it. He made the sun, the moon, and the stars. At last we could come to earth. We could have bodies of flesh and blood.

Hebrews 1:2; Abraham 4

Many people came to live on earth. Some of them were righteous. They obeyed God's commandments. Some people did not obey God. They were wicked.

MD, p. 157-8

9

Prophets taught the people about Heavenly Father's plan of salvation. They told the people about Jesus. He would come to earth to save the people.

Jacob 7:11; 2 Nephi 25:23-27

The prophets said Jesus would be born in Bethlehem. He would be the Son of God. His mother would be a good and beautiful woman. Her name would be Mary.

Micah 5:2; Mosiah 15:3; Isaiah 7:14; 1 Nephi 11:18-21

The prophets said many people would not know Jesus was the Savior. He would look like other people. He would not be rich. Many people would hate him.

Isaiah 53:2-3

Prophets also told about John the Baptist. He would come before Jesus. He would tell the people about Jesus. He would baptize Jesus.

Isaiah 40:3; Matthew 3:3; 1 Nephi 10:7-10; 11:27

Jesus would be very kind. He would do many miracles. He would suffer for the sins of all people who would repent.

Mosiah 3:5-8

Jesus Christ would be our Savior. He would be crucified. He would die on a cross.

Mosiah 15:7-9; Numbers 21:6-9; John 3:14

After three days Jesus would be resurrected. His spirit would come back into his body. Because Jesus died and was resurrected, we will be resurrected too.

Isaiah 5:8; 2 Nephi 2:8

The New Testament is the story of Jesus and his Apostles. They lived in Israel. People who lived in Israel were called Israelites or Jews. The Romans had captured Israel. The Roman king was the king of Israel.

ELISABETH AND ZACHARIAS

Chapter 1

Zacharias was an Israelite. He lived near Jerusalem. His wife was Elisabeth. They obeyed God's commandments. Zacharias and Elisabeth were old. They had no children. They prayed for a baby.

Luke 1:5-7, 13

Zacharias was a priest. He worked in the temple. One day an angel named Gabriel came to him. Zacharias was afraid. Gabriel told him not to be afraid. Gabriel said God would bless Elisabeth and Zacharias. God would answer their prayer. Elisabeth would have a baby. Gabriel said they should name the baby John.

Luke 1:8-13, 19

God had work for John to do. John would have the priesthood. He would tell people about Jesus Christ. John would be a righteous prophet of God.

Luke 1:15-17

Zacharias did not believe Gabriel. He said Elisabeth was too old to have a baby. Gabriel said God sent him to tell Zacharias it was true. Because Zacharias did not believe it, he would not be able to talk until John was born.

Luke 1:18-20

MARY AND THE ANGEL

Chapter 2

Mary and Joseph lived in Nazareth. They were righteous. They loved each other. They were going to be married.

Luke 1:26-27

One day the angel Gabriel came to Mary. He told Mary God loved her. He said Mary would be blessed more than any other woman. Mary was afraid. Gabriel told her not to be afraid. God loved her. She would be blessed.

Luke 1:26, 28-30

Gabriel told Mary she would have a baby boy. She should name him Jesus. The baby would be the Son of Heavenly Father. Jesus would be the king of all righteous people.

Luke 1:31-33

Mary did not have a husband. Gabriel said the boy's father would be Heavenly Father. The baby would be the Son of God. Mary said she would obey Heavenly Father. She would be the mother of Jesus.

Luke 1:34-35, 38; 1 Nephi 11:18-21

JOHN THE BAPTIST IS BORN

Chapter 3

The angel Gabriel told Mary that Elisabeth would have a baby boy. Mary and Elisabeth were cousins.

Luke 1:36-38

Mary went to visit Elisabeth. The Holy Ghost told Elisabeth that Mary would be the mother of Jesus Christ. Mary and Elisabeth thanked God for blessing them. They were filled with the Holy Ghost. Mary stayed with Elisabeth for three months. Then she went home to Nazareth.

Luke 1:39-56

Elisabeth's son was born. Elisabeth and her friends and family were happy. They thought the baby should have the same name as his father, Zacharias. But Elisabeth said his name would be John. Everyone was surprised.

Luke 1:57-61

The people asked Zacharias what the baby's name should be. Zacharias could not talk. He had not spoken since the angel Gabriel talked to him. He wrote a note. It said, "His name is John."

Luke 1:62-63

At last Zacharias could speak. He was filled with the Holy Ghost. He thanked God for the baby. He told the people Jesus would soon be born.

Luke 1:64, 67, 76

John would teach the people about Jesus. John would be a great prophet.

Luke 1:64, 67-79

JOSEPH AND THE ANGEL

Chapter 4

Joseph was a righteous man. He and Mary would soon be married. Then he learned that Mary was going to have a baby. He did not know what to do. He thought he should not marry her.

Matthew 1:18-19

One night an angel came to Joseph in a dream. The angel said Mary's baby was the Son of God. The angel told Joseph to marry her. Joseph should name the baby Jesus. Jesus would be the Savior of the world.

Matthew 1:20-21

Joseph obeyed the angel. Joseph and Mary were married.

Matthew 1:24-25

JESUS CHRIST IS BORN

Chapter 5

The king of the Romans made a law. He said everyone must pay taxes. Joseph and Mary lived in Nazareth. They had to go to Bethlehem to pay their taxes. Bethlehem was 65 miles from Nazareth.

Luke 2:1-5

It was not easy for Mary to travel to Bethlehem. Her baby would soon be born.

Luke 2:4-5

At last Joseph and Mary came to Bethlehem. Many people were there to pay their taxes. All the rooms were filled with people. Mary and Joseph needed a room. But there were no rooms left.

Luke 2:6-7

Mary needed a place to have her baby. So Joseph and Mary went to a stable. A stable is a place for animals. Joseph and Mary stayed in the stable. Mary had her baby there. She put warm blankets on the baby. She laid him in a manger. Joseph and Mary named the baby Jesus.

Luke 2:7, 21

There were shepherds in the fields near Bethlehem. They were taking care of their sheep. That night an angel came to the shepherds. The shepherds were afraid.

Luke 2:8-9

The angel told them not to be afraid. He came to tell them some wonderful news. The Savior was born in Bethlehem. They would find him in a manger. His name was Jesus Christ.

Luke 2:10-12

The shepherds went to Bethlehem. They saw the baby Jesus in a manger. Joseph and Mary were with him.

Luke 2:15-16

The shepherds left the stable. They were happy they had seen the Savior. They told other people what they had seen.

Luke 2:17, 20

THE WISE MEN

Chapter 6

There were some wise men who lived in another land. They knew what the prophets said about the birth of Jesus. They saw a new star in the sky. The star meant that Jesus was born.

Matthew 2:1-2

The wise men knew Jesus would be king. They went to see King Herod in Jerusalem. They asked King Herod where the new king was. Herod told the wise men to go to Bethlehem. They would find Jesus there.

Matthew 2:1-2, 8

The wise men went to Bethlehem. They saw Jesus and Mary. The wise men were very happy. They knelt down and worshiped Jesus. They gave him gifts. Then they went home.

Matthew 2:11-12

KING HEROD TRIES TO KILL JESUS AND JOHN THE BAPTIST

Chapter 7

King Herod was worried. The wise men said Jesus would be king. Herod did not want a new king. He wanted to be the only king. So he thought of a way to kill Jesus. He knew Jesus was a baby. He told his soldiers to kill all the babies in Bethlehem and the places nearby. Then Jesus would be killed.

Matthew 2:3, 13, 16

An angel visited Joseph. He told Joseph to take Mary and Jesus to Egypt. Egypt is far from Bethlehem. Herod would not find Jesus in Egypt.

Matthew 2:13

Joseph obeyed. He took Mary and Jesus to Egypt. They were in Egypt when Herod's soldiers killed all the babies at Bethlehem.

Matthew 2:14, 16

Zacharias did not want John to be killed. He sent Elisabeth and John to the mountains. John would be safe there.

TPJS, p. 261

King Herod asked Zacharias where John was. Zacharias would not tell Herod.

TPJS, p. 261

King Herod sent his soldiers to kill Zacharias. They killed him near the altar in the temple.

Matthew 23:35

Later King Herod died. Then an angel visited Joseph. He told Joseph to take Jesus and Mary home. Joseph took them to Nazareth. Jesus was safe there.

Matthew 2:19-21, 23

THE BOY JESUS

Chapter 8

Jesus lived in Nazareth when he was a boy. He learned many things. He prayed to his Heavenly Father. God loved Jesus.

Luke 2:39-40

When Jesus was 12, Joseph and Mary took him to Jerusalem. They stayed in Jerusalem for a few days.

Luke 2:41-43

Then Joseph and Mary left Jerusalem. They started home to Nazareth. But Jesus stayed in Jerusalem. Joseph and Mary did not know Jesus stayed in Jerusalem. They thought Jesus was walking home with his friends.

Luke 2:43-44

Joseph and Mary did not see Jesus all day. They looked for him. But they did not find him. No one knew where he was. So Joseph and Mary went back to Jerusalem to find him. They looked for Jesus for three days. They could not find Jesus. They were very sad.

Luke 2:44-46

At last they found Jesus in the temple. He was talking to some teachers. He was asking them questions. He was answering their questions.

The teachers were surprised Jesus knew the answers. Joseph and Mary were surprised, too.

Luke 2:46-47

27

Mary told Jesus she was worried about him. She and Joseph had looked for him for three days. Jesus said they should not worry about him. He said he was doing his father's work. God was his real father. Joseph and Mary did not understand what he meant.

Luke 2:48-50

Jesus went home to Nazareth with Joseph and Mary.

Luke 2:51

Jesus learned more and more about his Heavenly Father's work.

Luke 2:52

He grew tall and strong.

Luke 2:52

People loved him. He did what God wanted him to do.

Luke 2:52

God loved him.

Luke 2:52

JESUS IS BAPTIZED

Chapter 9

John lived in the desert for many years. He was called John the Baptist. He ate honey and grasshoppers. He wore clothes made out of camel's hair. People came from the cities to listen to John teach.

Matthew 3:1-5

John the Baptist taught the people about Jesus Christ. John told the people to repent of their sins. He told them to be baptized. John the Baptist baptized people in the water. They were baptized to wash away their sins.

Matthew 3:6

The people asked John the Baptist how to live better lives. He told them to share with poor people. He said they should always tell the truth. He told them not to hurt other people. John the Baptist told the people that Jesus Christ was coming to start his church. Jesus would give the Holy Ghost to them when he came. John the Baptist knew Jesus was the Savior. He told the people Jesus Christ was the Savior.

Luke 3:10-14; Matthew 3:2, 11-12; John 1:33-36

One day John the Baptist was baptizing people in the Jordan River. Jesus Christ went down to the river. He asked John the Baptist to baptize him. John the Baptist knew Jesus was righteous.

Jesus did not sin. He always obeyed God's commandments. He did not need to repent. So John thought Jesus did not need to be baptized.

Matthew 3:13-15; 2 Nephi 31:5-7

But God commanded all people to be baptized. Jesus told John the Baptist to baptize him. Jesus went into the water. John the Baptist baptized him. Jesus was baptized to obey God's commandment.

Matthew 3:16; 2 Nephi 31:7-8

When Jesus came out of the water, the Holy
Ghost came to him. God spoke from heaven.

God said, "This is my beloved Son."

Matthew 3:16-17

JESUS IS TEMPTED

Chapter 10

Jesus went into the wilderness to be with God. Jesus stayed in the wilderness for 40 days. He talked with God. Jesus fasted. He did not eat or drink anything.

Matthew 4:1-2; JST, Matthew 4:1

After 40 days the devil came to Jesus. The devil tempted Jesus three times. Three times he told Jesus to do bad things. First the devil told Jesus to change some rocks into bread. Jesus was hungry. He had power and could change rocks to bread. But he knew he should only use his power to help other people. So he did not do what the devil said. He did not change the rocks into bread. He obeyed God.

Matthew 4:2-4; JC, pp. 128-29

Then the Holy Ghost took Jesus to a high place on the temple. The devil came to Jesus again. He told Jesus to jump off the temple. The devil said angels would catch Jesus before he got hurt. The devil wanted Jesus to test Heavenly Father. He wanted Jesus to see if Heavenly Father would help him. But Jesus did not do what the devil said. Jesus did not jump. He would not test his Heavenly Father.

Matthew 4:5-7; JST, Matthew 4:5

Then the Holy Ghost took Jesus to the top of a mountain. The Holy Ghost showed Jesus all the kingdoms and money in the world. The devil came again. The devil said Jesus could have all the kingdoms and money if Jesus would obey him. Jesus said he would not obey the devil. Jesus said he would obey only his Heavenly Father. He told the devil to go away. The devil left Jesus. Then angels came and blessed Jesus. Now Jesus was ready to begin his work.

Matthew 4:8-11; JST, Matthew 4:8

JESUS AND HIS HEAVENLY FATHER'S HOUSE

Chapter 11

Jesus went to Jerusalem. He went to the temple. Many people went to the temple to make sacrifices. They made a sacrifice by killing an animal and burning it on an altar. The sacrifice helped people think about the Savior. He would suffer and die for them.

Leviticus 1:3-9; Moses 5:5-7; John 2:13

Some people did not have an animal to sacrifice. There were men who sold animals to them. The men sold the animals in the temple. They wanted to get money. They did not think about God.

John 2:14; DNTC, 1:137-8

Jesus saw the men selling the animals in the temple. He said the temple was his Heavenly Father's house. He wanted his Heavenly Father's house to be a holy place. Jesus did not want the men to sell things in his Heavenly Father's house.

John 2:16; DNTC, 1:137-8

Jesus made a whip. He made the men leave the temple. He threw the money on the floor. He turned over the tables. Jesus would not let the men sell animals in his Heavenly Father's house.

John 2:15-16

THE LEADER'S SON

Chapter 12

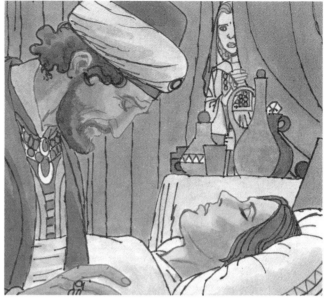

A leader of the people had a son. The son was very sick. He was about to die. Everyone thought he would die.

John 4:46-47

The leader left his son at home. He traveled many miles to find Jesus. He found Jesus in the city of Cana.

John 4:46-47

The leader asked Jesus to come and heal his son. He said his son would die if Jesus did not heal him. Jesus told the leader to go home. Jesus said the son would be healed. The leader had faith in Jesus. He went home.

John 4:47-50

The leader's servants came to meet him. They said his son was healed. The leader asked his servants what time his son began to get well.

They told him. It was the same time that Jesus said the son would be well.

John 4:51-53

The leader knew that Jesus healed his son. The leader and all his family had more faith in Jesus.

John 4:53

ANGRY PEOPLE IN NAZARETH

Chapter 13

Jesus went to Nazareth. Nazareth was the city where he grew up.

Luke 4:16

Jesus went to a Jewish church meeting. He stood up and read from the Bible. He read what the prophet Isaiah wrote. Isaiah said the Savior would come to earth. The Savior would help all people.

Luke 4:16-19

Jesus sat down after he read Isaiah's words. The Jews looked at Jesus. They did not know why he read Isaiah's words. They waited for Jesus to tell them why.

Luke 4:19-20

Jesus said Isaiah's words were about him. He was the Savior. The people were surprised. They did not believe Jesus was the Savior. They thought he was Joseph's son. They did not know he was the Son of God.

Luke 4:21-22

Jesus knew what the people were thinking. He knew they did not believe he was the Savior. He knew they wanted him to show them a miracle. But Jesus told them he would not. He would not do miracles for people who did not have faith.

Luke 4:23-27

The people were angry. They did not believe Jesus was the Savior. They took him up to the top of a hill. They wanted to throw him off the hill.

Luke 4:28-29

But they could not throw him off the hill. They could not hurt him. Jesus walked away from them.

Luke 4:30

JESUS CHOOSES HIS APOSTLES

Chapter 14

One day Jesus was at the Sea of Galilee. He was teaching the people. He was in a boat. A man named Peter was with him. The boat was Peter's. Peter and his friends had fished all night. They did not catch any fish.

Luke 5:1-5

Jesus finished teaching the people. He told Peter to take the boat into the deep water. Peter did what Jesus said. Then Jesus told Peter to put his fish nets in the water. Peter obeyed Jesus.

Luke 5:4-5

Peter and his friends put their fish nets in the water. The nets filled up with fish. The nets got so full they began to break.

Luke 5:5-6

Peter called to his friends in another boat. He asked them to come and help. The men put all the fish in the two boats. The fish filled both boats.

Luke 5:7

Peter and his friends were surprised. They had many fish. They knew Jesus made this happen.

Luke 5:9

Peter knelt down by Jesus' feet. Peter said, "I am a sinner." He was afraid. But Jesus told Peter not to be afraid.

Luke 5:8-10

Peter and his friends took their boats back to the land. Jesus told Peter and his friends to come with him. Two of Peter's friends were brothers. Their names were James and John. Peter, James, and John left everything they had. They went to help Jesus. Jesus asked other men to come with him, too.

Luke 5:10-11; Matthew 4:18-22; 9:9; John 1:35-51

Jesus needed 12 leaders for his church. They would be called Apostles. Jesus wanted to choose the right men. He prayed all night. The next morning he chose 12 men to be Apostles.

He ordained the 12 men. He gave them the priesthood. He gave them the power to be Apostles.

Luke 6:12-16; John 15:16

Jesus sent the 12 Apostles on missions. They traveled to many cities. The Apostles taught the gospel. They healed people. Then the Apostles came back to tell Jesus what they did.

Luke 9:1-6, 10; Mark 6:30

THE MAN WHO COULD NOT WALK

Chapter 15

Jesus was in a house. Many people were with him. He was teaching them the gospel.

Luke 5:17

Four men came to see Jesus. They were carrying a friend on a bed. The friend was very sick. He could not walk. The men wanted to take him to Jesus. But they could not get in the house. There were too many people.

Luke 5:18-19

The four men took the sick man up on the roof. They made a hole in the roof. They let the man down through the roof. They laid him in front of Jesus.

Luke 5:19.

Jesus knew that the men had great faith. He told the sick man to pick up the bed and go home. The man stood up. He was healed. He picked up his bed and walked home. He knew that Jesus healed him.

Luke 5:20, 24-25

THE SERMON ON THE MOUNT

Chapter 16

Jesus was up on a mountain by the Sea of Galilee. He was teaching some people the gospel.

Matthew 4:25; 5:1

He told them how to live so they could be happy. He told them how to go back to heaven. The things he said will make us happy too.

Matthe ̄

We should not think we are better than other people.

Matthew 5:5

We should try as hard as we can to be righteous.

Matthew 5:6

We should forgive people who hurt us or make us feel bad. If we forgive them, Heavenly Father will forgive us.

Matthew 5:7

We should love other people. We should help them love each other.

Matthew 5:9

We should not be afraid to tell other people about the gospel. We should tell them we love Heavenly Father. We should do good. When other people see us do good, they might believe in God too.

Matthew 5:14-16

We should always keep our promises. We should do everything we say we will do.

Matthew 5:33-37

We should be nice to other people. We want others to be nice to us. So we should be nice to them.

Matthew 7:12

Jesus said if we do these things we will be happy. God will bless us. We will be able to go back to heaven.

Matthew 5:2-12

JESUS TEACHES ABOUT PRAYER

Chapter 17

Jesus taught his disciples how to pray. He said some people pray on the street. They want others to see them praying. Jesus said people should pray where they can be alone.

Matthew 6:5-6

When some people pray, they say the same words over and over. They do not think about what they say. Jesus said people should not say the same words over and over when they pray. They should think about what they say. They should pray for things they need.

Matthew 6:7-8

51

Jesus showed the disciples how to pray. He said a prayer for them. He began his prayer by saying, "Our Father . . . in Heaven." He thanked Heavenly Father. He asked Heavenly Father for help. He said "Amen" at the end of his prayer. Later Jesus told his disciples to pray in his name. Then Heavenly Father would answer their prayers. If people pray, Heavenly Father will bless them.

Matthew 6:9-13; John 16:23; Luke 11:5-10; DNTC 1:233-37

JESUS FORGIVES A WOMAN

Chapter 18

A Pharisee asked Jesus to eat with him. Pharisees were leaders of the Jews. Jesus went into the Pharisee's house. He sat down to eat with the Pharisee.

Luke 7:36

A woman lived in the city. She had many sins. She knew that Jesus was eating at the Pharisee's house. She went to the house.

Luke 7:37

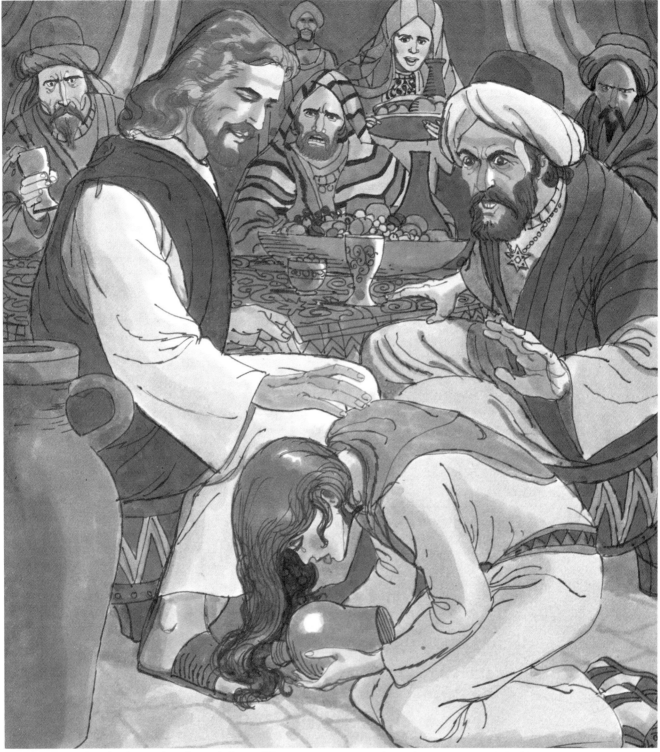

The woman knelt down by Jesus' feet. She was crying. She washed his feet with her tears. She dried them with her hair. She kissed his feet. She put sweet-smelling oil on them. The Pharisee saw what the woman did. He knew the woman had many sins. He thought Jesus should know the woman was a sinner. He thought Jesus should not let her touch him.

Luke 7:38-39

Jesus knew what the Pharisee was thinking. Jesus told the Pharisee to look at the woman. Jesus said the Pharisee gave him no water to wash his feet. But the woman washed Jesus' feet with her tears. She dried his feet with her hair.

The Pharisee did not kiss Jesus. But the woman kissed Jesus' feet many times. The Pharisee did not give Jesus oil. But the woman put sweet-smelling oil on Jesus' feet.

Luke 7:44-46

Jesus told the Pharisee the woman had many sins. But she had repented of her sins. She loved Jesus very much. She had faith in him. Jesus told the woman her sins were forgiven. He told her not to be sad any more.

Luke 7:47-50; DNTC 1:264-65

JESUS COMMANDS THE WIND AND THE WAVES

Chapter 19

One day Jesus and his disciples were in a boat on the Sea of Galilee. Jesus fell asleep. The wind began to blow very hard. The waves were high. They filled the boat with water. The disciples thought the boat would sink. They were afraid. They awoke Jesus and asked him to help.

Luke 8:22-23

Jesus stood up. He commanded the wind to stop blowing. He told the waves to go down. The wind stopped blowing. The waves went down.

Luke 8:24

Jesus asked the disciples why they were afraid. He said they should have more faith. The disciples were surprised and afraid. They wanted to know what kind of man Jesus was. He could tell the wind to stop. He could tell the waves to go down. The wind and waves obeyed him.

Luke 8:25

THE MAN WITH THE EVIL SPIRITS

Chapter 20

A man lived in the mountains by the Sea of Galilee. He had an evil spirit in him. The evil spirit made him act wild. The people tried to stop him. They tied him with ropes and chains. But he broke the ropes and chains.

Mark 5:1-4

The man spent all night and all day in the mountains and the caves. He cried all the time and cut himself with stones.

Mark 5:5

One day Jesus and his disciples crossed the Sea of Galilee in a boat. When Jesus came out of the boat, the man ran to him.

Mark 5:1-2, 6

Jesus told the evil spirit to come out of the man. The evil spirit knew who Jesus was. He called Jesus the Son of God. He asked Jesus not to hurt him.

Mark 5:7-8

Jesus asked the evil spirit what his name was. The evil spirit said, "My name is Legion." Legion means many. There were many evil spirits in the man. The evil spirits asked Jesus not to send them away. They saw some pigs. The evil spirits asked Jesus to send them into the pigs.

Mark 5:9-12

Jesus told them to leave the man and go into the pigs. There were 2,000 pigs. The evil spirits left the man and went into the pigs. The pigs ran down the hill into the sea and drowned.

Mark 5:13

The men who took care of the pigs ran to the city. They told many people what happened. The people came to see. They saw Jesus. They saw the wild man. But he was not wild anymore.

Mark 5:14-15

The people could not understand. Other people told them what happened. The people were afraid of Jesus. They asked him to go away. Jesus went back into the boat.

Mark 5:15-18

The man who was healed wanted to go with Jesus. Jesus told him not to come. He told the man to tell his friends what Jesus had done for him.

Mark 5:18-19

The man went to his friends. He told them what Jesus had done. They knew Jesus had great power.

Mark 5:20

A WOMAN TOUCHES JESUS' CLOTHES

Chapter 21

A woman was very sick. She had been sick for 12 years. She had been to many doctors. The doctors could not heal her.

Mark 5:25-26

She heard about Jesus. One day she saw Jesus. She knew she would be healed if she touched Jesus' clothes. There were many people around Jesus. She came behind him and touched his clothes.

Mark 5:27-28

The woman was healed. She was not sick any-more. Jesus turned around. He asked, "Who touched me?"

Mark 5:29-30

The woman was afraid. She knelt down by Jesus. She told him she had touched him. Jesus said her faith made her well.

Mark 5:33-34

JESUS FEEDS 5,000 PEOPLE

Chapter 22

Some friends of John the Baptist came to Jesus. They said John the Baptist had been killed. He was killed because he told the king to repent.

Matthew 14:1-12

When Jesus heard this, he went to the Sea of Galilee to be alone. But many people knew where he was. They came to hear him teach. There were more than 5,000 of them.

Matthew 14:13; Mark 6:44

Jesus taught the people. He taught them all day. He taught them until it was night.

Mark 6:34-35

Jesus' disciples wanted the people to go away. It was time to eat, and the people did not have any food. The disciples wanted them to go buy food.

Mark 6:36

Jesus told the disciples to feed the people. He told them to look for food. They found one boy with food. He had five loaves of bread and two fish.

Mark 6:37-38; John 6:9

Jesus told all the people to sit down. Jesus blessed the bread and the fish. He broke them in pieces.

Mark 6:39-41

The disciples took the pieces of food to the people. The people ate. There was more than enough food for all of them. This was a miracle.

Mark 6:41-44

JESUS WALKS ON THE WATER

Chapter 23

Jesus went up on a mountain to pray. His disciples went out on a boat on the Sea of Galilee. There was a big storm on the sea. The wind was blowing hard. The waves were high.

Matthew 14:22-24

Jesus came down the mountain in the night. He walked on the water to get to the boat.

Matthew 14:25

The disciples saw Jesus walking on the water. They were afraid. They thought he was a ghost. Jesus said, "It is I; be not afraid."

Matthew 14:26-27

Peter said he wanted to walk on the water. Jesus told Peter to walk to him. Peter climbed out of the boat. He began to walk on the water to go to Jesus.

Matthew 14:28-29

The wind was blowing hard. The waves were high. Peter was afraid. He began to sink into the water. He called to Jesus to save him.

Matthew 14:30

Jesus took hold of Peter's hand. He asked Peter why he was afraid. Jesus asked Peter why he did not have more faith.

Matthew 14:31

Jesus and Peter walked to the boat. The storm stopped. The disciples worshiped Jesus. They knew he was the Son of God.

Matthew 14:32-33

JESUS HEALS A DEAF MAN

Chapter 24

Some people brought a man to Jesus. The man was deaf. He could not hear. He could not talk very well. The people wanted Jesus to heal the man.

Mark 7:32

Jesus and the man walked away from the people. Jesus put his fingers in the man's ears. He touched the man's tongue. Jesus blessed him.

Mark 7:33-34

Then the man could hear and talk. The people could understand him. Jesus asked the people not to tell anyone what happened. But they told everyone.

Mark 7:35-36

THE BOY WITH AN EVIL SPIRIT

Chapter 25

One day some people came to Jesus and his disciples. One of the men asked Jesus to help his son. He had asked the disciples to heal his son. But they could not. The man's son had an evil spirit in him. The evil spirit made the boy hurt himself.

Mark 9:14-18

Jesus told the man to get his son. The boy came to Jesus. The evil spirit hurt the boy. It made him fall on the ground.

Mark 9:19-20

Jesus asked how long the evil spirit had been in the boy. The evil spirit had been in him since he was a child.

Mark 9:21

The father asked Jesus to heal the boy. Jesus told the boy's father to have faith. Jesus said he could heal the son if the father had faith. The father began to cry. He said he had faith.

Mark 9:23-24

Jesus commanded the evil spirit to come out of the boy. Jesus told the evil spirit never to go into the boy again. The evil spirit was angry. It hurt the boy again. Then it obeyed Jesus and came out of the boy.

Mark 9:25-26

The boy was very quiet. Many people said he was dead. But Jesus knew he was not dead. Jesus took hold of the boy's hand and helped him stand up. The boy was healed. The evil spirit was gone.

Mark 9:26-27

Later the disciples asked Jesus about the boy. They did not know why they could not make the evil spirit go out of him. Jesus told them they needed more faith to make the evil spirit go out. He said they should have fasted and prayed for faith.

Mark 9:28-29

JESUS HEALS A BLIND MAN

Chapter 26

One day Jesus was walking with his disciples. They saw a blind man. He was born blind. The disciples asked if he was blind because he sinned. They asked if his parents sinned.

John 9:1-2

Jesus said the blind man did not sin. His mother and father did not sin. The man was blind so that Jesus could heal him. Then people could see God's power.

John 9:3-5

Jesus made mud out of the dirt. He put mud on the blind man's eyes. He told the man to wash his eyes.

John 9:6-7

The blind man obeyed. He washed the mud out of his eyes. Then he could see.

John 9:7

His friends saw him. They thought he was someone else. He told them he was the blind man. He told them how Jesus had healed him.

John 9:8-11

The friends took the man to the Pharisees. He told the Pharisees Jesus healed him. Some of the Pharisees thought Jesus was a prophet. Other Pharisees hated Jesus. They were angry. They told the man to go away.

John 9:13-16, 28-34

Jesus found the man. Jesus asked the man if he had faith. The man said yes. He worshiped Jesus.

John 9:35-38

THE GOOD SHEPHERD

Chapter 27

Jesus called himself the good shepherd. A shepherd takes care of sheep. He helps them find food and water. He does not let them get hurt or lost. He knows them and loves them. He would give his life to save his sheep.

John 10:11-15

Jesus is like a shepherd to people. He loves them. He helps them learn the truth. He shows them how to get to heaven. Jesus called his people his sheep. He gave his life for them.

John 10:11-15

Jesus told the people in Jerusalem that he had other sheep. The people in Jerusalem did not know what Jesus meant. Jesus meant that he had disciples in America. He said he would visit them.

John 10:16; 3 Nephi 15:21

After Jesus was resurrected in Jerusalem, he visited his other disciples. They were the people in America. The Book of Mormon tells about them. Jesus stayed many days with the Book of Mormon people. He loved them. He blessed them and healed the sick. He gave them the priesthood. He started his Church. He taught them the same things he taught the people in Jerusalem. Then he went back to his Heavenly Father.

3 Nephi 11-28

THE GOOD SAMARITAN

Chapter 28

Jesus told many stories. He told stories to teach people. The stories helped them learn the truth.

One day a leader of the Jews came to Jesus. The leader wanted to trick Jesus. He asked Jesus how to get into heaven. Jesus asked the leader what the scriptures said. The leader said a man should love God. He should also love his neighbor. Jesus said the leader was right. Then the leader asked Jesus. "Who is my neighbor?"

Luke 10:25-29

Jesus told the leader a story. A Jew was walking on a road. Some thieves stopped him. They took his clothes. They beat him. They left him on the road. He was almost dead.

Luke 10:30

Soon a Jewish priest came by. He saw the man who was hurt. The priest should have helped him. But he did not. The priest walked by on the other side of the road. He left the man alone.

Luke 10:31

Then another Jewish man came along the road. He worked in the temple. He saw the man who was hurt. He also should have helped him. But he did not. He walked by on the other side of the road. He left the man alone.

Luke 10:32

Then a Samaritan came along. The Samaritans were not Jews. The Jews and the Samaritans did not like each other. The Samaritan saw the man who was hurt. He knew the man was a Jew. But he felt sorry for him. The Samaritan took care of the man. The Samaritan put clothes on him.

Luke 10:33-34; John 4:9; DNTC 1:151

The Samaritan took the Jew who was hurt to an inn. He took care of him until the next day. Then the Samaritan had to leave. He gave money to the man who owned the inn. He told him to take care of the hurt man.

Luke 10:34-35

This was the story Jesus told the leader of the Jews. Then Jesus asked which of the three men was the man's neighbor.

Luke 10:36

The leader said the Samaritan was the neighbor because he helped. Then Jesus told the Jewish leader to be like the Samaritan.

Luke 10:37

JESUS TELLS THREE STORIES

Chapter 29

One day Jesus was eating and talking with some sinners. Some Pharisees came to talk to Jesus.

Luke 15:1-2

The Pharisees thought they were good men. They did not talk to sinners. They thought Jesus should not talk to sinners.

Luke 15:2

Jesus wanted to teach the Pharisees they were wrong. He wanted them to know why he was with the sinners. He told them three stories. The first story was about a lost sheep.

Luke 15:3; TPJS, p. 277

THE LOST SHEEP

The First Story

A good shepherd had 100 sheep. One of the sheep was lost.

Luke 15:4

The good shepherd left the other 99 sheep. He went to look for the lost one. He wanted to save it. He found the lost sheep. He was very happy.

Luke 15:4-5

He picked it up and put it on his shoulders. He carried it home. When the shepherd got home, he called to all his friends and neighbors. He told them to come and be happy with him. He had found the sheep that was lost.

Luke 15:5-6

Jesus told the Pharisees what the story meant. Jesus said he is like the good shepherd in the story. Sinners are like the lost sheep.

Luke 15:7

The shepherd wanted to save the lost sheep. Jesus said he wants to save sinners.

Mark 2:17

The shepherd was very happy when he found the lost sheep. Jesus said he is happy when sinners repent.

Luke 15:6-7

That was why Jesus was talking with sinners.

JST, Matthew 18:11; Mark 2:17; DNTC, 1:508-09

THE LOST COIN

The Second Story

A woman had ten silver coins. Coins are pieces of money. The woman lost one coin. She looked all through the house for it.

Luke 15:8

At last the woman found the lost coin. She was very happy. So she called her friends and neighbors. They were happy, too, because the woman found the lost coin.

Luke 15:9

The friends and neighbors in the story were like angels. The angels of God are very happy when a sinner repents.

Luke 15:10; DNTC, 1:508-11

Jesus said he is like the woman in the story. The lost coin is like a sinner. Jesus wants to find the sinners. He wants to help them repent. Jesus is very happy when a sinner repents.

Luke 15:10; DNTC, 1:509

THE LOST SON

The Third Story

A man had two sons. Each son would get some money when the father died. The younger son asked for his part of the money. He did not want to wait until his father died. He wanted the money then. The father gave the younger son the money.

Luke 15:11-12

The son took the money and left home. He went to another land. He spent all his money. He sinned. He did not obey God's commandments.

Luke 15:13

He had no money to buy food. He was very hungry. He asked a man for help.

Luke 15:14-15

The man sent him to feed the pigs. The son was so hungry he wanted to eat the pigs' food. He thought of his family. He knew everyone at home had enough to eat. Even the servants had enough to eat. He wanted to go home. But he knew he had sinned. He had not obeyed God's commandments. He had not obeyed his father. He thought he was not good enough to be a son. But he wanted to repent. He would ask to be a servant in his father's house.

Luke 15:15-19

The son went home. His father saw him coming.

Luke 15:20

The father loved his son. He ran to meet him. He put his arms around him and kissed him.

Luke 15:20

The son said he had sinned. He had not obeyed God's commandments. And he had not obeyed his father.

Luke 15:21

The father told a servant to bring good clothes. The servant put the clothes on the son. He put shoes on his feet. He put a ring on his finger.

Luke 15:22

The father told the servant to make a big dinner. He wanted everyone to eat and be happy. His son had gone away, but now he was home. His son had sinned, but now he had repented.

Luke 15:23-24

The older son had been working in the field. When he came home, he heard music and dancing. He asked a servant what was happening. The servant said the younger son had come home. Their father wanted everyone to eat and be happy.

Luke 15:25-27

The older son was angry. He would not go into the house. His father came out to talk to him.

Luke 15:28

The older son said he had worked many years for his father. He always obeyed his father. But his father had never given him a big dinner. He asked why his father had a big dinner for the younger son. The younger son was a sinner.

Luke 15:29-30

The father said the older son had always stayed with him. He had not gone away. Everything the father had would belong to the older son. The father said it was good to have a dinner for the younger son. His younger son had gone away, but now he was home. His son was a sinner, but he had repented.

Luke 15:31-32

Jesus ended the story. He had told the Pharisees three stories. The stories showed the Pharisees why Jesus was talking to sinners. Jesus wanted the Pharisees to know how much Heavenly Father loves everyone. Heavenly Father loves people who obey him. He also loves sinners. He wants sinners to repent so they can come back to him.

John 3:16-17

THE TEN LEPERS

Chapter 30

Jesus went to a small town. He saw ten sick men. They were lepers. They had sores all over their bodies. Their skin was falling off.

Luke 17:12

Doctors could not help the lepers. People did not like to go near them. They did not want to get sick, too.

Luke 17:12

The lepers asked Jesus to heal them. They knew that Jesus could make their sores go away.

Luke 17:13

Jesus listened to the lepers. He wanted them to be well. He told them to go to the priests. The lepers obeyed Jesus. They went to the priests.

Luke 17:14

On their way to the priests, the ten lepers were healed. Their sores were gone. Jesus had healed them.

Luke 17:14

One of the lepers came back to thank Jesus. He knew Jesus had healed them. He knelt down. He thanked Jesus for making him well. Jesus asked where the other nine lepers were. They had not come back to thank him. Jesus said the leper's faith had made him well.

Luke 17:15-19

THE PHARISEE AND THE PUBLICAN

Chapter 31

One day Jesus talked to some people. They thought they were righteous. They thought they were better than other people. They hated other people. Jesus did not want them to think they were better than other people. So he told them a story.

Luke 18:9

Two men went to the temple to pray. One was a Pharisee. The other was a publican. People had to pay tax money to the publicans. Sometimes the publicans took too much money. The people did not like the publicans.

Luke 18:10

The Pharisee stood up to pray. He thanked God he was better than other men. He said he fasted two times each week. He paid more tithing than other people. The publican stood by himself. His prayer was not like the Pharisee's prayer. The publican bowed his head to pray. He was sorry for his sins. He asked God to forgive him.

Luke 18:11-13

Jesus said the Pharisee thought he was better than other men. The Pharisee thought he had no sins. He thought he did not need help from God. Jesus said the publican knew he had sinned. The publican wanted to repent. He prayed that God would forgive him. He wanted to be more righteous.

Luke 18:14

Jesus said the publican would be forgiven. The Pharisee would not. Jesus said people should be like the publican. They should not think they are better than other people. They should repent of their sins. They should ask God to forgive them. They should try to be more righteous.

Luke 18:14

JESUS BLESSES THE CHILDREN

Chapter 32

Jesus was with his disciples. Some people wanted Jesus to bless their children. The disciples told the people not to bring their children to Jesus.

Mark 10:13

Jesus told the disciples to let the children come to him. He told the disciples they should be like little children. Children love Jesus very much.

The disciples should have faith like little children. Then they could live with God in Heaven.

Mark 10:14-15

THE RICH YOUNG MAN

Chapter 33

One day a young man came to Jesus. The young man was very rich. He asked Jesus what he should do to get to heaven.

Mark 10:17, 22

Jesus told him to obey God's commandments. Jesus said the young man should not kill. He should not lie or steal. Jesus told him to love his father and mother. The rich young man said he always obeyed those commandments.

Mark 10:18-20

Jesus loved the young man. He wanted to help him. Jesus said the young man needed to do one more thing. He must sell everything and give the money to the poor people and follow Jesus. Then he could go to heaven.

Mark 10:21

The rich young man was very sad. He did not want to give away everything he had. He loved his money more than he loved God. He left Jesus.

Mark 10:22

Jesus told his disciples it is hard for a rich man to go to heaven. The disciples did not understand. They asked who can live with God. Jesus said people who love God can live with him. Men must love God with all their hearts. Then they will go to heaven.

Mark 10:23, 26, 29-30

THE WIDOW'S MITES

Chapter 34

Jesus was by the temple in Jerusalem. He was watching the people give money to the Church. The people were putting their money into big boxes. Jesus saw many rich men put a lot of money into the boxes.

Mark 12:41

A poor woman came to the boxes. Her husband had died. She was a widow. She put in two pieces of money called mites. Two mites were not very much money. But the two mites were all the money she had.

Mark 12:42, 44

Jesus saw her. Jesus wanted to teach his disciples a lesson. He told them about the widow.

Mark 12:43

Jesus told his disciples the rich men gave lots of money. But the rich men had more money at home.

Mark 12:43

The widow had only two mites. She had no money at home. She gave all her money to the Church. She had given more to the Church than all the rich men.

Mark 12:44

95

THE TEN YOUNG WOMEN

Chapter 35

Ten young women went to a wedding. They waited at the door for the bridegroom. The bridegroom was the man getting married. The bridegroom would let them in. No one knew when the bridegroom would come to open the door.

Matthew 25:1, 13

The ten women had lamps. The lamps burned oil to make light. Five of the women were wise. They had oil in their lamps. They also had more oil with them.

Matthew 25:2, 4

The other five women were not wise. They had only the oil that was in their lamps.

Matthew 25:3

The bridegroom did not come for a long time. All the oil in the lamps was gone. The five wise women put more oil in their lamps. The other five women had to go buy more oil.

Matthew 25:5-9

While they were gone, the bridegroom came. He let the five wise women in the door. They went to the wedding.

Matthew 25:10

The other five women came back. The door was closed. They could not go to the wedding.

Matthew 25:11-13

97

Jesus told this story to help members of the Church. Jesus is like the bridegroom. Jesus will come to earth again. His coming will be like the wedding. The members of the Church are like the ten women. Some members of the Church will be like the wise women. They will be ready for Jesus to come. They will be able to be with the Savior. Other members will be like the five women who needed more oil. They will not be ready when the Savior comes. They will not be able to go with the Savior. Wise members of the Church obey God's commandments. They will be ready when Jesus comes again.

DNTC, 1:684

THE TALENTS

Chapter 36

Jesus told his disciples a story. A man gave his servants some talents. A talent is a piece of money.

Matthew 25:14-15

The man gave one servant five talents. He gave another servant two talents. He gave another servant one talent. Then the man went to another land.

Matthew 25:15

The servant with five talents worked hard. He made five more talents. Then he had ten talents.

Matthew 25:16

The servant with two talents worked hard. He made two more talents. Then he had four talents.

Matthew 25:17

But the servant with one talent was not like the other servants. He hid his talent. He buried it in the ground. He was afraid he would lose it. He did not make any more talents.

Matthew 25:18

The man came home. He asked the servants what they had done with their talents.

Matthew 25:19

The first servant brought ten talents to the man. The servant had worked hard. The man was happy. He made the servant a leader over many things. He told the servant to be happy.

Matthew 25:20-21

The second servant brought four talents to the man. The servant had worked hard. The man was happy. He made the servant a leader over many things. He told the servant to be happy.

Matthew 25:22-23

The third servant came to the man. He had only one talent. The servant gave the talent to the man. The man was not happy with the servant. He said the servant was lazy. The servant should have worked hard. Then he would have had more talents.

Matthew 25:24-27

The man took the talent from the servant. He gave the talent to the servant with ten talents. The man sent the lazy servant away.

Matthew 25:28-30

JESUS BRINGS LAZARUS BACK TO LIFE

Chapter 37

A man named Lazarus lived in Bethany. He lived with his sisters, Mary and Martha. They loved Jesus very much.

John 11:1-2

Lazarus became very sick. Jesus was teaching in another town. Mary and Martha sent a man to tell Jesus Lazarus was sick. Jesus loved Lazarus and his sisters.

John 11:3

Jesus wanted to help Lazarus. Jesus asked his disciples to go with him. The disciples were afraid. Bethany was near Jerusalem. Some of the people in Jerusalem wanted to kill Jesus. The disciples did not want Jesus to go near Jerusalem again.

John 11:6-8

Jesus told his disciples Lazarus was dead. Jesus would bring him back to life. His miracle would help the disciples know Jesus was the Savior. Jesus went to Bethany.

John 11:9-17; JC, p. 491; DNTC, 1:530-31

Lazarus had been dead four days. Martha went to meet Jesus. She said Lazarus would not have died if Jesus had been there. Jesus told Martha Lazarus would live again. Jesus asked Martha if she believed him. Martha said yes. She knew Jesus was the Savior.

John 11:17-27

Then Martha left Jesus. She went to get her sister Mary. Mary went to meet Jesus. Many people went with her. Mary knelt at Jesus' feet.

She was crying. The people with her were crying, too. Jesus cried. The people said that he loved Lazarus very much.

John 11:28-36

They took Jesus to the cave where Lazarus was buried. There was a stone in front of the cave. Jesus told the people to move the stone.

John 11:38-39

Jesus looked up. He prayed to Heavenly Father. He thanked Heavenly Father for hearing his prayers. He asked Heavenly Father to help the people believe in him. He wanted the people to know he was the Savior.

John 11:41-42

Then Jesus spoke in a loud voice. He told Lazarus to come out of the cave. Lazarus came out. He was alive again. The people saw the miracle. They knew Jesus was the Savior. They believed in him.

John 11:43-45

THE SAVIOR GOES TO JERUSALEM

Chapter 38

Some people went to the Pharisees. They told the Pharisees Jesus had brought Lazarus back to life. The Pharisees thought everyone would believe in Jesus. They thought no one would listen to them any more.

John 11:46-48.

The Pharisees wanted Jesus to die. They planned a way to kill Jesus. They thought Jesus would come to Jerusalem for the Passover dinner. They waited for him.

John 11:50-51, 56-57

Jesus came from Bethany to Jerusalem. Many people heard he was coming. They went out to meet him. Jesus was riding a young donkey. A prophet had written that the Son of God would ride a young donkey into Jerusalem. Many people believed in Jesus. The people knew Jesus was the Son of God. They had seen his miracles. They put their clothes on the ground for the donkey to walk on. They waved palm leaves in the air. They said Jesus was the Savior.

John 12:1, 12-15; Zechariah 9:9; Matthew 21:4-9

All the people in Jerusalem came to see what was happening. They asked who Jesus was. The disciples said he was a prophet from Nazareth.

Matthew 21:10-11

The Pharisees saw Jesus. They were angry because many people believed him. Jesus knew the Pharisees wanted to kill him.

John 12:19, 23; 11:53-54

Jesus told his disciples he would soon die. He knew he would suffer for the sins of all people. He knew he would die on the cross. He would be the Savior of the world. This was why he came to earth.

John 12:23-25, 27, 32-33, 47

THE FIRST SACRAMENT

Chapter 39

Every year the Jews had a dinner. It was called the Passover dinner. This dinner helped them remember how God saved the Israelites in Egypt. God saved them long ago in the time of Moses.

Exodus 12:27; 13:15; Luke 22:7

Jesus and his 12 Apostles needed a place to eat the Passover dinner. Jesus sent Peter and John to get a room ready for the dinner.

Luke 22:8

They found the room and got the dinner ready.

Luke 22:9-13

Jesus and the Apostles went to the room. They ate the Passover dinner.

Luke 22:14

After dinner Jesus gave his Apostles the sacrament for the first time. He took some bread in his hands and blessed it. Then he broke the bread into pieces. He told the Apostles to eat the bread.

Luke 22:19; Matthew 26:26

Jesus told them to think of his body when they ate the bread. They should remember that he would die for them.

Luke 22:19; Matthew 26:26

Jesus poured some wine into a cup. He blessed the wine. He told the Apostles to drink it.

Matthew 26:27

Jesus told them to think of his blood when they drank the wine. They should remember that he would bleed and suffer for them. He would bleed and suffer to take away people's sins.

Luke 22:20; Matthew 26:28

Jesus told the Apostles that some wicked men would kill him. The Apostles were very sad. They loved the Savior. They did not want him to die. Jesus knew that Judas would help the wicked men. Judas was one of the Apostles.

Matthew 26:2, 14-16, 21-25

Then Jesus and the Apostles sang a song and left the room. They walked to the garden called Gethsemane. Judas did not go with them. He went to the Pharisees.

Matthew 26:30, 36, 47

110

JESUS SUFFERS IN THE GARDEN OF GETHSEMANE

Chapter 40

Jesus and the Apostles went to the Garden of Gethsemane.

Matthew 26:36

Jesus went into the Garden to pray. He asked Peter, James, and John to go with him. He told them to wait while he prayed.

Matthew 26:36-38

Jesus began to pray. He asked Heavenly Father to bless him. Jesus did not want to suffer. But he wanted to obey Heavenly Father. He would suffer for all people who repent of their sins.

Matthew 26:39-44

Peter, James, and John went to sleep while Jesus was praying. Jesus saw them sleeping. He asked them to stay awake.

Matthew 26:40-41

Jesus went back to pray again. Peter, James, and John wanted to stay awake. They were sorry that Jesus was suffering so much. But they were very sleepy. They went to sleep again. Jesus came again and saw them sleeping. He went back to pray.

Matthew 26:42-43

Jesus was praying. He was sad. He began to shake. Blood came out of his skin. All his body hurt. It hurt because he was suffering for the sins of all people. While Jesus suffered and prayed, an angel came to make him stronger. Jesus finished praying. He had bled and suffered for the sins of all people.

Luke 22:42-44; D&C 19:16-18

Jesus went to Peter, James, and John. He woke them. Jesus told them he would be killed by wicked men. The men were coming to get him.

Matthew 26:45-46

JESUS IS CRUCIFIED

Chapter 41

Some wicked men came into the garden. The Pharisees had sent them. The men had swords and sticks.

Matthew 26:47

Judas, the Apostle, was with them. The men had paid Judas to find Jesus. They did not know which man Jesus was.

Matthew 26:14-16, 47

Judas told the men he would kiss Jesus. Then they would know who Jesus was. Judas came and kissed Jesus.

Matthew 26:48-49

The men took Jesus to the Pharisees. The Pharisees could not kill Jesus themselves. Only the Romans could kill Jesus.

Matthew 26:57, 59; Matthew 27:1

The Pharisees took Jesus to Pilate. Pilate was the Roman leader in Jerusalem. The Pharisees told Pilate that Jesus should die. Pilate asked Jesus many questions. He did not think Jesus had done anything wrong.

Matthew 27:2, 11-13; Luke 23:14

Pilate told the Pharisees Jesus had done nothing wrong. Pilate wanted to let Jesus go. But the Pharisees hated Jesus. They said to Pilate, "Crucify him! Crucify him!" Pilate did not want trouble with the Pharisees. So he told his soldiers to crucify Jesus.

Luke 23:13-24; John 19:6

Pilate's soldiers took Jesus and beat him with whips. They made fun of Jesus. They made a crown of thorns. They put it on his head. The thorns hurt his head and made it bleed. The soldiers put a purple robe on Jesus. They laughed at him and spit on him. They called him the king of the Jews.

Mark 15:15-19

The soldiers took Jesus to a hill near Jerusalem. Many Jews followed. The soldiers crucified Jesus. They laid him on the wooden cross. They nailed his hands and his feet to the cross. Then they lifted up the cross. They also crucified two other men. The two other men were thieves.

Luke 23:26-27, 33

Jesus prayed. He asked his Heavenly Father to forgive the soldiers who crucified him. They did not know he was the Savior.

Luke 23:24

Jesus' mother, Mary, was standing by the cross. The Apostle John was standing there too. Jesus told John to take care of his mother. He told his mother to go with John.

John 19:25-27

Jesus' disciples were very sad. They loved Jesus very much. Jesus suffered on the cross many hours. Then Jesus died. His spirit left his body.

Matthew 27:46, 50; Luke 23:27-28

The sky was dark. There was a big earthquake. Rocks broke in pieces. The curtain in the temple was torn in half. The Roman soldiers were afraid.

Matthew 27:45, 51, 54

One of Jesus' disciples took Jesus' body off the cross. He wrapped Jesus' body in a cloth and put it in a tomb. A tomb is a place where people are buried. He put a big rock in front of the tomb.

Matthew 27:57-60

JESUS IS RESURRECTED

Chapter 42

Jesus' body was in the tomb three days. On Sunday morning two angels came from heaven. They moved the rock away from the tomb.

JST, Matthew 28:2

A woman named Mary Magdalene came to the tomb. She was a friend of Jesus. She saw that the rock was not in front of the tomb. Jesus' body was not in the tomb.

John 20:1-2

Mary Magdalene ran to find Peter and John. She told them someone had taken Jesus' body. She did not know where it was.

John 20:2

Peter and John ran to the tomb. John looked into the tomb. He saw the cloth Jesus was buried in. But Jesus was not there.

John 20:3-7

Peter and John did not know what had happened to Jesus. They went home. Mary Magdalene stayed by the tomb. She was crying. She looked into the tomb. The two angels were in the tomb.

John 20:9-12

The angels asked Mary Magdalene why she was crying. She said someone had taken Jesus' body away. She did not know where it was.

John 20:13

Mary Magdalene turned around and saw Jesus. She did not know he was Jesus. She thought he was the gardener. Jesus asked Mary Magdalene why she was crying. He asked who she was looking for. Mary Magdalene still thought he was the gardener.

John 20:14-15

Jesus said. "Mary." Then Mary Magdalene knew
he was Jesus. He asked her to tell the Apostles
he was resurrected.

John 20:16-17

Mary Magdalene went to the Apostles. She told them what Jesus had said. She told them she had seen Jesus. He was resurrected. The Apostles did not believe her.

John 20:18; Luke 24:11

Later the Apostles were talking to each other. Jesus came into the room. The Apostles were afraid. They thought Jesus was dead.

Luke 24:36-37

Jesus asked why they were afraid. He told them to touch his hands and feet. Jesus was resurrected. His body and spirit had come together again. He was alive again.

Luke 24:38-40

The Apostles were happy to see Jesus. He asked them for some food. They gave him some fish and some honey. He ate it.

Luke 24:41-43

Jesus was the first person to be resurrected. Many other people were resurrected after Jesus. Many people saw them.

Matthew 27:52-53

THE APOSTLES LEAD THE CHURCH

Chapter 43

After he was resurrected, Jesus came to his Apostles. He stayed with them for 40 days. He taught them many things about his Church.

Acts 1:1-3

Jesus told his Apostles to teach the gospel to all people. He told them he would leave them soon.

But the Holy Ghost would come to help them.

Acts 1:4-8

Then Jesus went to his Heavenly Father. The Apostles watched him go up to heaven. Two men in white clothes came and stood by the Apostles. The men told the Apostles Jesus would come back some day. He would come again out of heaven.

Acts 1:9-11

The Apostles were the leaders of the Church on earth. Peter was the president. James and John were his counselors. But there were only 11 Apostles. Judas was dead.

Matthew 27: 3-5; Matthew 16:18-19; D&C 81:1-2

The Apostles had to choose another Apostle. Heavenly Father told them whom to choose. They chose Matthias. There were 12 Apostles again. They had the priesthood.

Acts 1:15-26; D&C 102:8-9

The Apostles and the Saints had faith. They obeyed God's commandments. They loved one another.

Acts 2:41-47

The Apostles had the power of the Holy Ghost. They could do many things. They healed sick people. They taught about Jesus. They taught the gospel. They were missionaries. Many people believed the Apostles and joined the Church. The people who joined the Church were called Saints.

Acts 2:2-4; 29-43, 47; 3:7; Romans 1:7

PETER HEALS
A MAN

Chapter 44

One day Peter and John saw a man by the door of the temple. He could not walk. His friends had to carry him everywhere he went. Every day he sat by the temple doors. He asked people for money.

Acts 3:1-2

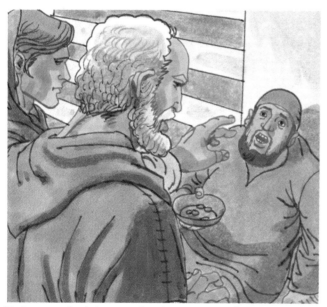

Peter and John walked over to the man. He asked them for some money. Peter said he did not have any money. He said he would give the man something else.

Acts 3:3-6

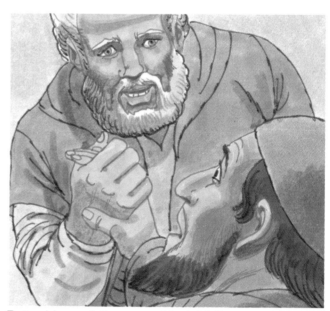

Peter blessed the man. He told the man to stand up and walk. Peter healed him in the name of Jesus Christ. Peter helped the man stand up.

Acts 3:6-7

The man began to walk. He walked for the first time in his life. Many people saw the man walking and jumping. They knew it was a miracle. They knew Peter had the power of God. Peter told them Jesus Christ gave him the power to heal the man. Peter helped many people believe in Jesus Christ. Peter was a great missionary.

Acts 3:8-13; 4:4

SIMON AND THE PRIESTHOOD

Chapter 45

Many people in Samaria heard the gospel. They believed the gospel and were baptized. But they did not have the Holy Ghost.

Acts 8:5, 12-16

Peter and John went to Samaria. They put their hands on the people's heads and gave them the Holy Ghost.

Acts 8:14-17

A man named Simon was in Samaria. He saw Peter and John give people the Holy Ghost. Simon knew Peter and John had power. They had the priesthood. The priesthood gave them power. Simon wanted the power of the priesthood.

Acts 8:9, 18:19

He asked them if he could buy the priesthood. Peter told Simon no one can buy the priesthood. God gives the priesthood to men. Only righteous men can have the priesthood. Peter knew Simon was not righteous. He told Simon to repent. Simon would not repent. He did not get the priesthood.

Acts 8:18-24

133

PETER BRINGS TABITHA BACK TO LIFE

Chapter 46

A woman named Tabitha lived in a city called Joppa. She was a very good woman. She helped many people. They loved her.

Acts 9:36-39

One day she became very sick. She died.

Acts 9:37

Her friends were very sad. They went to see Peter. They asked him to come and bless Tabitha. Peter went with them.

Acts 9:38-39

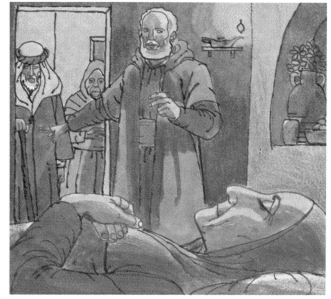

Peter saw Tabitha. He asked her friends to leave the room.

Acts 9:39-40

He knelt down and prayed. Then he told her to stand up. She opened her eyes and saw Peter.

Acts 9:40

Peter took hold of her hand. He helped her stand up. He told her friends to come back into the room. Her friends saw that Tabitha was alive.

They were happy. Peter brought Tabitha back to life. This was a miracle.

Acts 9:41-42

THE PHARISEES KILL STEPHEN

Chapter 47

Many of the Pharisees were afraid of the Apostles. They thought miracles would stop when Jesus died. But the Apostles did miracles like Jesus did. Many people believed in Jesus and joined the Church.

Acts 4:1-2, 13-17; 5:14

Many people made trouble for the Church. The leaders of the Jews put Peter and John in prison. The king had the Apostle James killed.

Acts 4:3; Acts 12:1-2

The Apostles called other men to help lead the Church. One of these men was Stephen. He was a righteous man. He was filled with the Holy Ghost. He did many miracles. He taught the gospel to many people.

Acts 6:3-10

Stephen told the Pharisees they were wicked. He said they killed Jesus Christ, the Son of God.

Acts 7:51-52

The Pharisees were angry. They took Stephen out of the city to kill him. They laid their coats by a young Pharisee named Paul. They threw stones at Stephen to kill him.

Acts 7:57-58

Stephen was dying. He looked up into heaven. He was filled with the Holy Ghost. He saw Heavenly Father and Jesus. He asked Jesus to take his spirit to heaven. Then he died.

Acts 7:55-56, 59-60

PAUL LEARNS ABOUT JESUS

Chapter 48

Paul was a Pharisee. He watched the people kill Stephen. One day Paul was going to a city named Damascus. He was with some friends. They were going to put more Saints in prison.

Acts 7:58; 9:1-2

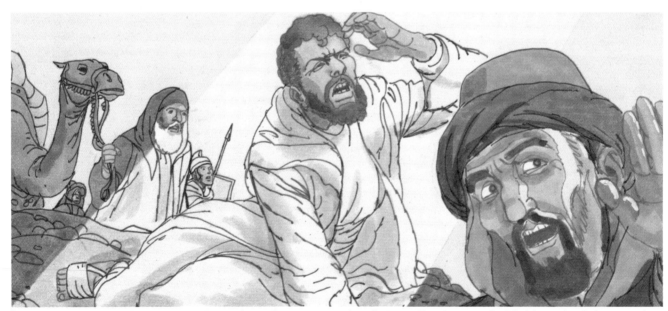

Suddenly a bright light came down from heaven. The light was all around Paul. He fell to the ground. He heard the voice of Jesus from heaven. Jesus asked why Paul was trying to hurt the Saints. Paul was afraid. He asked Jesus what to do. Jesus told him to go to the city. Paul would be told what to do.

Acts 9:3-6

Paul got up. He opened his eyes, but he could not see. He was blind. His friends took him into Damascus.

Acts 9:8-9

A disciple named Ananias lived in Damascus. He had a vision. In the vision Jesus told Ananias to go to Paul.

Acts 9:10-11

Ananias had the priesthood. He put his hands on Paul's head and healed him. Paul could see. Then Ananias baptized Paul and gave him the Holy Ghost.

Acts 9:17-18

Paul became a missionary for the Church. He wrote many letters. He went to many lands and taught the gospel. When some of the other Apostles were killed, Paul was chosen to be an Apostle.

Acts 26:16-23; Romans 1:1

PAUL AND SILAS IN PRISON

Chapter 49

There was a girl with an evil spirit in her. People liked to hear what the evil spirit said. There were some men with the girl. People paid the men to hear the evil spirit.

Acts 16:16

Paul and his friend Silas were teaching the gospel. The girl followed them. Paul told the evil spirit to leave her. The men were angry at Paul. Now that the evil spirit was gone, they could not make any more money.

Acts 16:7-19

The men took Paul and Silas to the leaders of their city. The men lied to the leaders. They said Paul and Silas were doing wicked things. The leaders believed the men.

Acts 16:20-22

The people became angry. They whipped Paul and Silas and put them in prison.

Acts 16:22-24

That night Paul and Silas prayed. They sang songs to Heavenly Father. All the men in the prison heard them. Suddenly the ground began to shake. The prison shook. The doors of the prison opened.

Acts 16:25-26

The guard woke up and saw the open doors. He thought the men in the prison had run away. But Paul told him all the men were there. The guard knew God had made the ground shake and the prison doors open. The guard knelt down by Paul and Silas. He asked how he could be saved.

Acts 16:27-30

Paul told him to believe in Jesus Christ. Paul and Silas taught the gospel to him. They took him out of the prison and baptized him. They also baptized his family.

Acts 16:31-33, 40

Then Paul and Silas went back to the prison. The next day the leaders let Paul and Silas out of the prison. Paul and Silas went to another city to do more missionary work.

Acts 16:34-36

142

PAUL OBEYS THE HOLY GHOST

Chapter 50

The Holy Ghost told the Apostle Paul to go to Jerusalem. The Holy Ghost said Paul would be put in prison. Some wicked men would hurt him. But Paul had missionary work to do. He was not afraid. He loved the Savior. He would go to Jerusalem.

Acts 20:22-24

Paul said good-bye to his friends. He said he would never see them again. He told them to obey God's commandments. He told them to remember the gospel. He knew wicked men would try to teach them bad things. He told them not to listen.

Acts 20:25, 28-32

He told them to love each other and take care of each other. He knelt down and prayed with them. All of them cried. They hugged Paul and kissed him. They went with him to the boat. Paul went to Jerusalem.

Acts 20:35-38; 21:1-15

PAUL FINISHES HIS MISSION

Chapter 51

Paul went to the temple in Jerusalem. He took some people who were not Jews into the temple. The Jews were angry. They took Paul out of the temple and whipped him.

Acts 21:26-32

Some Roman soldiers took Paul away from the Jews. Paul asked if he could talk to the Jews. He said he was a missionary teaching the gospel of Jesus Christ. He said he had seen a light from heaven. He had heard the voice of Jesus.

Acts 21:31-40, 22:1-21

The Jews did not believe Paul. They shouted at him. They wanted to kill him. The soldiers put Paul in prison for the night.

Acts 22:22-30, 23:1-10

That night Jesus came to Paul. He told Paul not to be afraid. Jesus said Paul would go to Rome. Paul would teach the gospel in Rome.

Acts 23:11

The Jews wanted the Romans to kill Paul. So they sent him to King Agrippa. Agrippa was a Roman king. Agrippa asked what Paul had done. Paul said he had been a Pharisee. He had hated the people who believed in Jesus. He had put them in prison. One day he saw a light from heaven. He heard the voice of Jesus. Then he believed in Jesus.

Acts 23:12-35; 25:13-23; 26:1-15

Paul said Jesus had told him to teach the gospel of Jesus Christ. The Jews hated Paul because he taught about Jesus. Paul told Agrippa the gospel was true. Paul said Jesus was resurrected.

Acts 26:16-26

King Agrippa said he almost believed in Jesus because of what Paul said. Paul wanted King Agrippa and all people to believe in Jesus. That was why Paul was a missionary. King Agrippa did not think Paul should be killed. He sent Paul to Rome.

Acts 26:27-32; 27:1-2

Paul was in prison in Rome for two years. Many people came to see Paul. He taught them the gospel. He wrote letters to the Saints in other lands. Many of these letters are in the New Testament.

Acts 28:16-31

Paul knew he would be killed. But he was not afraid. He had obeyed God's commandments. He had taught the gospel. He had finished his mission. He knew Heavenly Father loved him. He knew he would live with Heavenly Father and Jesus after he died. Later Paul was killed.

2 Timothy 4:6-8

AFTER THE NEW TESTAMENT

Peter, James, and John and the other Apostles worked hard. They were good missionaries. They taught about Jesus Christ. They helped many people join the Church. There were Saints in many lands. The Saints tried to obey God's commandments. But wicked people did not want them to believe in Jesus.

Acts 6:2-4; 7; 11:19-21

The wicked people tried to change the commandments. They did not want the Saints to obey God's commandments. Some Saints believed the wicked people. They stopped believing in Jesus. They did not obey God's commandments.

Titus 1:10-11; Galatians 1:6-8; 1 John 2:18-19

Many righteous Saints were killed. The Apostles were killed. There was no one to lead the Church. The Church of Jesus Christ was not on the earth anymore. The people were not righteous enough to have the gospel. Peter, Paul, and many other prophets had said that would happen.

Matthew 23:34; 24:8-10; Romans 8:36; 1 Peter 4:12;
1 Corinthians 4:9-13; JC, 745-6

Hundreds of years went by. There were many different Churches. But they did not have Apostles. Their leaders did not have the priesthood. The churches were not the Church of Jesus Christ. But the prophets said that after many years the Church of Jesus Christ would be on the earth again.

2 Timothy 4:3-4; 2 Thessalonians 2:1-4; Acts 3:19-26

A boy named Joseph Smith wanted to know which church was the Church of Jesus Christ. He went into the woods near his home. He knelt down and prayed. He asked God to tell him which church to join.

Joseph Smith — History 5, 10, 14-15

Heavenly Father and Jesus came to Joseph Smith. Jesus told Joseph not to join any of the churches. The Church of Jesus Christ was not on the earth. Jesus chose Joseph Smith to help start the Church again.

Joseph Smith — History 17-19

God chose Joseph Smith to be a prophet. Angels gave Joseph Smith the priesthood. He translated the Book of Mormon.

Joseph Smith—History 33, 66-75

God chose 12 Apostles to lead the Church. They had the power to teach the gospel and do miracles. The Church of Jesus Christ was on the earth again.

D&C 107:22-23; 102:3

God sent missionaries to tell all people about the Church of Jesus Christ. The Doctrine and Covenants tells about these things.

D&C 1:18, 30

The Church is the same church that Jesus and his Apostles had when they lived on earth. It is called The Church of Jesus Christ of Latter-day Saints.

D&C 115:4

WORDS TO KNOW

A

altar People pray at an altar. People burn animals on an altar.

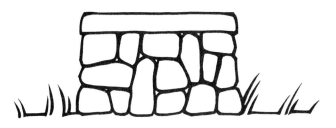

angel An angel is one of God's helpers from heaven. An angel talked to Mary.

Apostle An Apostle is a leader of Christ's church. Jesus chose 12 Apostles. Peter, James, and John were Apostles.

B

baptize Jesus asked John the Baptist to baptize him.

baptized When people join the Church, they are baptized. When people are baptized, their sins are washed away.

baptizing John the Baptist was baptizing people in the Jordan River.

believe To believe means to think something is true. Heavenly Father wants people to believe in him.

believed Many people believed in Jesus. Many people thought Jesus was the Son of God.

bleed When people bleed, blood comes out of their bodies. The thorns in Jesus' head made his head bleed.

bled Jesus bled in the Garden of Gethsemane.

bless To bless means to give good things. Peter went to bless Tabitha.

blessed Jesus blessed the children.

blessing Mary and Elisabeth thanked God for blessing them.

bodies of flesh and blood We had only spirit bodies in heaven. We got bodies of flesh and blood when we came to earth.

born Jesus was born to Mary. John the Baptist was born to Elisabeth. Jesus was Mary's baby, and John was Elisabeth's baby.

bowed The publican bowed his head to pray.

bridegroom A bridegroom is a man getting married.

buried A person is buried after he dies. Jesus was buried in a tomb.

C

camel's hair Camel's hair is the hair from a camel. John the Baptist wore clothes made of camel's hair.

captured The Romans captured Israel. The Romans became the leaders in Israel.

153

cave A cave is a hole in a hill. Lazarus was buried in a cave.

chains The people tied the man with ropes and chains.

choose To choose means to pick the thing we want. Jesus had to choose 12 Apostles.

chose The Apostles chose Matthias to take Judas' place.

chosen Satan wanted to be chosen by Heavenly Father.

Church The Church is a grcup of people who believe in God. Many people joined the Church.

coin A coin is a piece of money. The woman lost a coin.

commanded Jesus commanded the wind to stop.
Jesus told the wind to stop.

commandments Good people obey God's commandments.
Good people do what God says they should do.

counselors James and John were Peter's counselors. James and John helped Peter lead the Church.

cousins Cousins are your aunt and uncle's children. Mary and Elisabeth were cousins.

cross Jesus was nailed on a cross.

crossed Jesus and his disciples crossed the Sea of Galilee in a boat.
Jesus and his disciples went to the other side of the Sea of Galilee in a boat.

crown The soldiers put a crown of thorns on Jesus' head.

crucify To crucify means to kill someone by putting him on a cross.
Pilate told his soldiers to crucify Jesus.

crucified Jesus was crucified on a cross.

D

desert A desert is dry land. John the baptist lived in the desert.

devil   Devil is another name for Satan.

disciple   A disciple is a person who follows Jesus and wants to be like him. Jesus taught his disciples.

dream   God spoke to Joseph in a dream. God spoke to Joseph while Joseph was asleep.

drowned   The pigs drowned in the sea. The pigs died in the sea because they could not swim.

E

earthquake   An earthquake is a strong shaking of the earth. The earthquake broke rocks.

evil spirit   An evil spirit is a bad spirit.

F

faith   We must have faith in Jesus Christ. We must believe and obey Jesus Christ.

fast   To fast is to go without food and water.

fasted   Jesus fasted for 40 days and 40 nights.

filled with the Holy Ghost   Mary and Elisabeth were filled with the Holy Ghost. The Holy Ghost helped them.

followed   The people followed Jesus. The people went where Jesus went.

forever   Forever means always. We can live with Heavenly Father forever if we keep his commandments.

forgive   To forgive means to forget the bad things someone has done. Jesus asked Heavenly Father to forgive the soldiers who crucified him.

forgiven   Jesus told the woman her sins were forgiven. Her sins were taken away.

G

ghost   The disciples thought Jesus was a ghost. The disciples thought Jesus was not a real person. They thought he was just a spirit.

gifts   Gifts are good things that people give to others. The wise men gave gifts to Jesus.

gospel   The gospel is what Jesus teaches us to do. We believe the gospel of Jesus Christ.

grasshopper   A grasshopper is an insect that jumps.

guard   A guard is a soldier who watches people in prison.

H

heal   To heal means to make sick people well. The people wanted Jesus to heal the deaf man.

healed   Jesus healed sick people. Jesus made sick people well.

heaven   Heavenly Father lives in heaven. Jesus taught us how to get to heaven.

holy   Something that is holy belongs to God. The temple is holy.

I

inn   An inn is a place to eat and sleep. It is like a hotel. The Samaritan took the Jew to an inn.

J

join the Church To join the Church means to believe in God and be baptized. Paul joined the Church.

K

knelt The woman knelt down to worship Jesus. The woman got on her knees to worship Jesus.

L

lamps Lamps give light so we can see.

lazy The servant was lazy.
The servant would not work.

lead To lead means to show people what to do. The Apostles helped lead the Church members.

leader The Apostles were the leaders of the Church.

legion Legion means many.

leper A leper is a sick person with sores all over his body. Jesus healed ten lepers.

lie Jesus told us not to lie.
Jesus told us not to say things that are not true.

lied The wicked men lied.

loaves Jesus fed 5,000 people with five loaves of bread.

M

manger A manger is a box for animal's food. Jesus was laid in a manger when he was a baby.

members The people were members of the Church.
The people were baptized and belonged to the Church.

miracle A miracle is something God can do that people cannot. People can do miracles with God's help.

missions The Apostles went on missions.
The Apostles went to other lands to tell people about the gospel of Jesus Christ.

missionary Paul was a missionary for the Church. Paul taught people about the Church.

mites The widow gave two mites.
The widow gave two pieces of money.
The two mites were not very much money.

mount A mount is a mountain. Jesus stood on a mount and taught the people.

N

neighbor   Jesus said a man should love <u>his neighbor</u>. Jesus said a man should love <u>everyone he knows</u>.

note   Zacharias wrote a <u>note</u>.
Zacharias wrote <u>some words on a paper</u>.

O

obey   To <u>obey</u> means to do what we are told to do. We should <u>obey</u> God's commandments.

obeyed   Joseph <u>obeyed</u> the angel. Joseph did what the angel told him to do. He took Mary and Jesus to Egypt.

ordained   Jesus <u>ordained</u> 12 men.
Jesus <u>gave the priesthood</u> to 12 men.

owned   The man <u>owned</u> the inn. The inn belonged to the man.

P

palm leaves   The people waved <u>palm leaves</u> in the air. They waved leaves from a <u>palm tree</u>.

Passover dinner   Jesus came to Jerusalem for <u>the Passover dinner</u>.
Jews ate the <u>Passover dinner to</u> remember that God saved the Israelites at the time of Moses.

power   Jesus gave the Apostles <u>power</u>.
Jesus gave the Apostles <u>help from God</u>.

pray   To pray means to talk to God. I <u>pray</u> to God every day.

prayed   Jesus <u>prayed</u> to God.

prayers   Jesus said many <u>prayers</u> to God.

praying   Peter, James, and John went to sleep while Jesus was <u>praying</u>.

president   Peter was <u>the president</u> of the Church.
Peter was the <u>most important leader</u> of the Church.

priests   The lepers went to <u>the priests</u>.
The lepers went to <u>the leaders of the Church</u>.

priesthood   <u>The priesthood</u> is the power of God. Jesus gave <u>the priesthood</u> to the Apostles.

prison   A <u>prison</u> is a place where people are put and cannot get out.
Paul was in <u>prison</u>.

promises   We should keep our <u>promises</u>. We should do everything we will say we will do.

prophet   A <u>prophet</u> tells us what God wants us to know.

prophets   God speaks to <u>prophets</u>.

publican   A <u>publican</u> is a man who takes the people's taxes.

R

repent   If we do something bad, we should <u>repent</u>.
If we do something bad, we should <u>feel sorry and not do it again</u>.
The publican wanted to <u>repent</u>.

157

repented The son had sinned, but now he repented.

resurrected Jesus Christ was resurrected. His spirit came back to his body. He is alive. He will never die again.

righteous To be righteous means to do what is right. Righteous people obey God's commandments.

S

sacrament Jesus gave his 12 Apostles the first sacrament.
Jesus gave his 12 Apostles some bread and some wine.
The sacrament helps us remember Jesus.

sacred The book is sacred. The book is from God.

sacrifice To sacrifice is to kill an animal and burn it on an altar.

sacrifice A sacrifice is the animal that has been killed and is burned on the altar.

Saints Saints are people who belong to Jesus' Church.

save Jesus died to save us.
Jesus died so we could go back and live with God.

saved God saved the Israelites in Egypt.
God kept the Israelites from being killed.

scriptures The scriptures are the words of God written in books.

sermon Jesus gave a sermon about the gospel.
Jesus taught the people about the gospel.

servant A servant is someone who works for someone else.

share To share means to give other people part of what we have.
John the Baptist told people to share with poor people.

shepherd A shepherd takes care of sheep.

sink To sink means to go under the water. Peter began to sink into the water.

sins Sins are the bad things we do. To kill and to steal are sins.

sinned The boy sinned. He did not obey God's commandments.

sinner A sinner is a person who does not obey God's commandments.

soldiers The soldiers obeyed the king.

sores Sores are places on the skin that hurt. The lepers had sores all over their skin.

spirit A spirit does not have a body of flesh and blood.

spirits We were spirits when we lived with Heavenly Father.

spirit bodies We had spirit bodies in heaven.

spirit children We are the spirit children of God.

stable A stable is a place for animals. Mary and Joseph stayed in a stable.

steal To steal means to take something that is not yours without asking. Jesus told us not to steal.

storm There was a storm on the sea. The wind blew hard and the waves were high.

suffer Jesus had to suffer for the sins of all people.
Jesus had to bleed and hurt for the sins of all people.

suffered Jesus suffered for the sins of all people.

suffering The Apostles were sorry that Jesus was suffering.

T

talents Talents are pieces of money. A man gave his servant five talents.

taxes The Jews paid taxes to the Romans.
The Jews paid money to the Romans.

temple A temple is God's house. We worship God in the temple.

tempt Satan and his evil spirits tempt us.
Satan and his evil spirits tell us to do bad things.

tempted The devil tempted Jesus three times.

tested God put us on earth to be tested.
God put us on earth to see if we would obey his commandments.

thieves Thieves are people who steal things. Some thieves took a man's clothes and money.

thorns The soldiers made a crown of thorns for Jesus. Thorns are sharp, and they hurt.

tithing Tithing is money we give to God.

tomb A tomb is a place where people are buried. Jesus was buried in a tomb.

torn The curtain in the temple was torn in half.

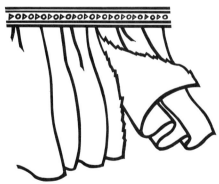

translated Joseph Smith translated the Book of Mormon.
Joseph Smith wrote the Book of Mormon in words we know.

travel To travel means to go from one place to another.

traveled The Apostles traveled to many cities.

traveling One day Jesus was traveling to Jerusalem.

truth Jesus teaches people the truth.
Jesus teaches people what is right.

V

vision A vision is a dream from God. Ananias had a vision.

voice Paul heard the voice of Jesus. Paul heard Jesus speak.

W

wedding People get married at a wedding.

whips The soldiers beat Jesus with whips.

wicked Wicked means bad. Some wicked men killed Jesus.

widow A widow is a woman whose husband has died.

wilderness A wilderness is a place where there are no cities or people.
Jesus went into the wilderness to be with God.

wise The five young women were wise.
The five young women were ready.

wise men The wise men knew Jesus would be born.

worshiped The disciples worshiped Jesus.
The disciples loved Jesus and obeyed his commandments.

PEOPLE TO KNOW

Agrippa Agrippa was a Roman King in Israel. Paul told Agrippa about Jesus Christ.

Ananias Ananias lived in Damascus. He healed Paul and gave him the Holy Ghost.

devil The devil is Satan. He tried to get Jesus to do bad things. He tries to get all people to sin.

Elisabeth Elisabeth was Zacharias' wife. She was the mother of John the Baptist.

Gabriel Gabriel was the angel who said Zacharias and Elisabeth would have a son. Gabriel told Mary and Joseph that Jesus would be the son of Heavenly Father.

God Heavenly Father, Jesus Christ, and the Holy Ghost are all Gods. They all have great power. We often call our Heavenly Father God.

Heavenly Father Heavenly Father is the father of our spirit bodies. He lives in heaven. We pray to Heavenly Father. Sometimes we call him God.

Herod Herod was a wicked king in Jerusalem. He tried to kill the baby Jesus.

Holy Ghost The Holy Ghost works with Heavenly Father and Jesus Christ. He has power to help people know the truth. The Holy Ghost has a spirit body. He does not have a body of flesh and bone.

Isaiah Isaiah was a prophet in Israel in Old Testament times. He said that Jesus would come to earth and help all people.

Israelites Israelites were people who lived in Israel. They were from the families of the 12 tribes of Israel. Jesus was an Israelite.

James James was one of Jesus' 12 Apostles. He was a counselor to Peter after Jesus went to heaven.

Jesus Christ Jesus Christ is the Son of God. He is the Savior. He suffered and died for us.

Jews Jews were people who lived in Israel. They were Israelites. Jesus was a Jew. Many Jews hated Jesus.

John John was one of Jesus' 12 Apostles. He was a counselor to Peter after Jesus went to heaven.

John the Baptist John the Baptist was the prophet who baptized Jesus. He was the son of Zacharias and Elisabeth.

Joseph Joseph was a righteous Jew. He was Mary's husband. He took good care of Mary and Jesus.

Judas Judas was one of Jesus' 12 Apostles. He helped the wicked men who wanted to kill Jesus.

Lazarus Lazarus was a friend of Jesus. Lazarus died. Jesus brought him back to life.

Mary Mary was the mother of Jesus. She was a righteous, beautiful woman.

Mary Magdalene Mary Magdalene was a friend of Jesus. She saw Jesus after he was resurrected.

Mary and Martha Mary and Martha were the sisters of Lazarus. They were friends of Jesus.

Matthias Matthias became one of the 12 Apostles after Jesus died.

Paul Paul was a Pharisee who hated Jesus' disciples. Paul learned the truth about Jesus and became an Apostle.

Peter Peter was one of Jesus' 12 Apostles. He was President of the Church after Jesus went to heaven.

Pharisees The Pharisees were leaders of the Jews. They hated Jesus and his disciples. The Pharisees asked the Romans to kill Jesus.

Pilate Pilate was a Roman leader in Jerusalem. He told his soldiers to crucify Jesus.

Romans The Romans captured Israel before Jesus was born. The Roman king was the king of Israel.

Samaritans The Samaritans were people who lived in Israel. The Jews and the Samaritans hated each other.

Satan Satan is a spirit son of Heavenly Father. He did not obey Heavenly Father, so he was sent out of heaven. Satan tries to get people to sin. Satan is the devil.

Savior   Jesus Christ is the Savior. He died to take away our sins. Because he was resurrected, we will be resurrected and live forever.

Silas   Silas was a missionary. Silas helped Paul teach the gospel.

Simon   Simon lived in Samaria. He wanted to buy the priesthood from Peter and John.

Son of God   Jesus Christ is the Son of God. Heavenly Father is his father. The Son of God is the Savior.

Stephen   Stephen was a righteous leader of the Church of Jesus Christ. The Pharisees killed Stephen.

Tabitha   Tabitha lived at Joppa. She died. Peter brought her back to life.

Zacharias   Zacharias was the father of John the Baptist. King Herod's soldiers killed Zacharias.

PLACES TO KNOW

America America was a land Jesus Christ visited after he was resurrected. Jesus had disciples in America.

Bethany Bethany was a town near Jerusalem. Lazarus and his sisters, Mary and Martha, lived in Bethany.

Bethlehem Bethlehem was a city near Jerusalem. Jesus was born in Bethlehem.

Cana Cana was a town near Nazareth. A man with a sick son came to Jesus in Cana.

Damascus Damascus was a city near Israel. Ananias healed Paul and gave him the Holy Ghost in Damascus.

Earth Earth is the place where we live now. Jesus Christ made the earth for us.

Egypt Egypt was a land far from Israel. Joseph took Mary and Jesus to Egypt so King Herod's soldiers could not kill Jesus.

Garden of Gethsemane The Garden of Gethsemane was near Jerusalem. Jesus prayed and suffered for the sins of all people in the Garden of Gethsemane.

Heaven Heaven is the place where Heavenly Father lives. We lived in heaven before we came to earth.

Israel Israel was the land where the Jews or Israelites lived. Jesus lived in Israel.

Jerusalem Jerusalem was a city in Israel. Jesus and his Apostles went to Jerusalem many times. Jesus was crucified and resurrected at Jerusalem.

Joppa Joppa was a city in Israel. Peter brought Tabitha back to life at Joppa.

Jordan River The Jordan River was in Israel. John the Baptist baptized Jesus in the Jordan River.

Nazareth Nazareth was the city where Mary and Joseph lived. Jesus grew up in Nazareth.

Rome Rome was a city far away from Israel. King Agrippa sent Paul to Rome.

Samaria Samaria was in Israel. Simon tried to buy the priesthood from Peter and John in Samaria.

Sea of Galilee The Sea of Galilee was a lake where Jesus and his Apostles went often. Jesus walked on the water of the Sea of Galilee.

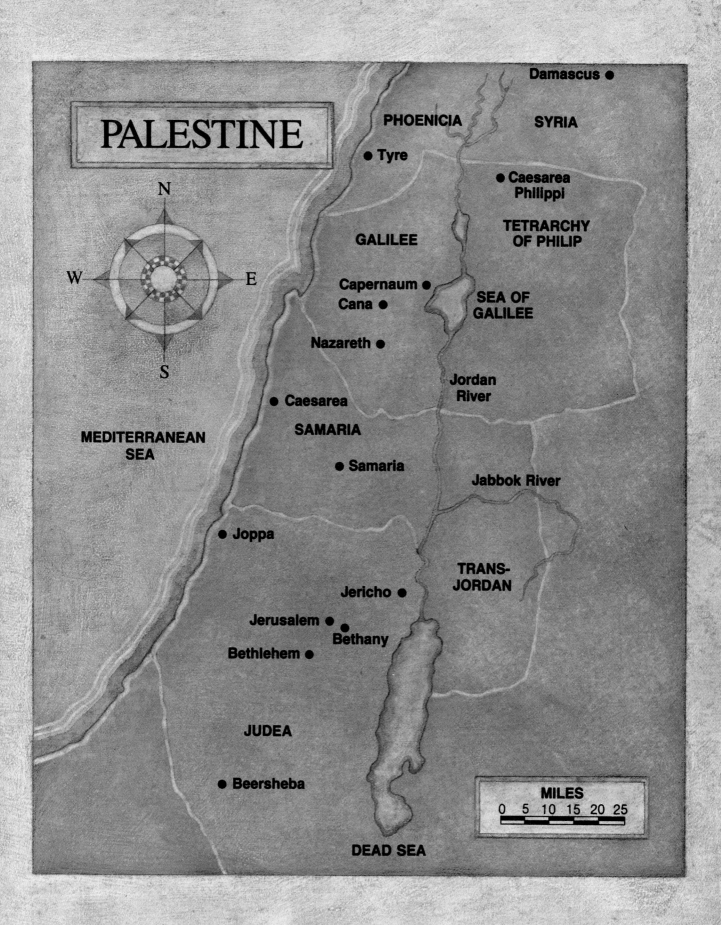

PALESTINE

N
W   E
S

Damascus ●

PHOENICIA   SYRIA

● Tyre

● Caesarea
Philippi

GALILEE   TETRARCHY
OF PHILIP

Capernaum ●

Cana ●   SEA OF
GALILEE

Nazareth ●

Jordan
River

● Caesarea

SAMARIA

MEDITERRANEAN
SEA

● Samaria

Jabbok River

● Joppa

TRANS-
JORDAN

Jericho ●

Jerusalem ●
    ● Bethany

Bethlehem ●

JUDEA

● Beersheba

MILES
0   5   10   15   20   25

DEAD SEA

Comments and Suggestions

Your comments and suggestions about this manual are appreciated. Please submit them to—

Curriculum Planning and Development
Floor 24
50 East North Temple Street
Salt Lake City, Utah 84150
USA

Identify yourself by name, address, ward, and stake. Then identify the name of the manual, how you used it, your feelings regarding its strengths and weaknesses, and any recommended improvements.